You Are in Tudor Times

Ivan Minnis

Raintree

www.raintreepublishers.co.uk
Visit our website to find out more information about **Raintree** books.

To order:
☎ Phone 44 (0) 1865 888112
🖹 Send a fax to 44 (0) 1865 314091
💻 Visit the Raintree Bookshop at **www.raintreepublishers.co.uk** to browse our catalogue and order online.

First published in Great Britain by Raintree, Halley Court, Jordan Hill, Oxford OX2 8EJ, part of Harcourt Education.
Raintree is a registered trademark of Harcourt Education Ltd.

Editorial: Nick Hunter and Catherine Clarke
Design: Michelle Lisseter, Richard Parker and Celia Floyd
Illustrations: Jeff Edwards
Picture Research: Maria Joannou and Ginny Stroud-Lewis
Production: Kevin Blackman

Originated by Dot Gradations Ltd
Printed and bound in China by South China Printing Company

ISBN 1 844 43288 2 (hardback)
08 07 06 05
10 9 8 7 6 5 4 3 2

ISBN 1 844 43293 9 (paperback)
09 08 07 06 05
10 9 8 7 6 5 4 3 2 1

British Library Cataloguing in Publication Data
Minnis, Ivan
You are in Tudor Times. – (You Are There)
942'.05
A full catalogue record for this book is available from the British Library.

Acknowledgements
The publishers would like to thank the following for permission to reproduce photographs:
AKG Images pp. **11**, **13** (British Library), **16** (Erich Lessing), **18** (British Library), **25**; Alamy Images (Ivan J. Belcher/Worldwide Picture Library) p. **4**; Ancient Art and Architecture pp. **5** (R. Sheridan), **6**, **7** (R. Sheridan), **10** (R. Sheridan), **19** (R. Sheridan), **21**, **27**; Bridgeman Art Library pp. **15** (Longleat House, Wiltshire), **22** (Leeds and Art Galleries/Temple Newsam House), **26** (National Portrait Gallery); Britain on View p. **8**; Corbis (Adam Woolfitt) p. **28**; Fotomas Index p. **12**; Glasgow University Library p. **23**; Mary Evans Picture Library p. **17**; National Trust Photolibrary pp. **9** (Derrik E. Witty), **20** (Angelo Hornak); The Royal Collection p. **24**; Trevor Clifford p. **14**.

Cover photograph of Little Moreton Hall, Cheshire, reproduced with permission of Philip Bratt.

Contents

Any words appearing in bold, **like this**, are explained in the Glossary.

Tudor times

England was a very different place 500 years ago. The country was controlled by a king or queen who made all the laws. People often fought each other to become the king or queen, also called the **monarch**. In 1485, King Richard III was beaten by his enemy, Henry Tudor. Henry became King Henry VII. His family ruled England and Wales until 1603 – nearly 120 years.

This was a very important time in English history. Many changes took place and England would never be the same again. The people of Tudor England lived in exciting times.

Chester was an important Tudor town. Many of the buildings from Tudor times are still standing today.

Tudor kings and queens

Henry VII	1485–1509
Henry VIII	1509–1547
Edward VI	1547–1553
Mary	1553–1558
Elizabeth I	1558–1603

Queen Elizabeth I is one of the most famous English monarchs in history. This portrait gives us an idea of what she looked like.

Elizabethan England

In this book you will travel back to the time of Queen Elizabeth I, the greatest of all the Tudor monarchs. She ruled from 1558 to 1603 and is famous for her power and wisdom. You will walk through England's busy towns and cities, visit the theatre and see how different life was for the rich and poor.

Tudor towns

Imagine yourself in Tudor London. London is the biggest and busiest city in Tudor England. The streets are narrow and lined with three- or four-storey houses. The upper storeys of the houses are bigger than the lower storeys. They hang over the streets, blocking out the light. The houses are **timber framed**. Fire can spread quickly through these narrow streets.

The River Thames is a busy place in Tudor London. Lots of people travel by river to avoid the narrow, crowded streets.

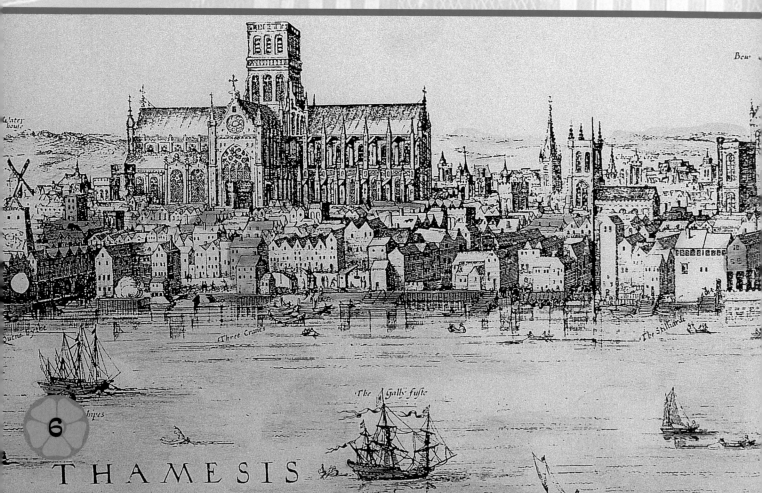

The streets are very smelly and slippery. Houses do not have toilets so people empty their **chamber pots** into the streets. The dirty streets attract rats, which spread **disease**. As you walk through the streets you will hear the shouts of shopkeepers calling out their prices. Watch out for robbers, too – they might attack you for your money. Tudor London can be a dangerous place.

It is easier to travel on the river than through the dirty and crowded streets. If you travel up the River Thames you might see one of the beautiful royal **barges** used by Queen Elizabeth.

Merchants like this one do deals on the streets of Tudor towns.

Meet the rich

As you walk through the streets of any Tudor town, you can see many types of people. Rich and poor people are dressed very differently. Rich people often travel in carriages, which block up the narrow streets.

Fine clothes

Rich men and women wear very fine clothes. The men usually wear a linen shirt under a jacket called a doublet. Another jacket is worn on top.

Rich people live in huge houses like Longleat House in Wiltshire.

Instead of trousers, they wear stockings and padded **breeches**. Many wear huge starched collars called ruffs.

The women wear many layers of clothes. Most wear a dress hoop called a **farthingale**. This is a frame that makes the skirt stick out for nearly 50 centimetres all around. It makes it very hard to sit down! Some women use a mixture of lead and vinegar on their faces to make them look pale. This make-up is **poisonous**.

Even the rich are a bit smelly. People say that Queen Elizabeth is one of the cleanest women in England because she has a bath once a month!

Life for the poor

Poor people do not look nearly as grand as the rich. Most poor men wear similar clothes to the rich, but they are much less colourful. The women cannot wear **farthingales** as they have to work hard and large dresses would get in their way. They try to copy the fashions of the rich women, using rough wool instead of fine silk. When children reach the age of five, they wear the same style of clothes as the adults.

Pedlars travel around, hoping to find people who will buy their goods.

Being too sick to work, means no money for food. Many poor people are forced to beg.

Sturdy beggars

There are many beggars and **vagabonds** in the city. Some are old and sick. If they are too sick to work, they have no money to buy food. Others roam the streets and countryside begging people to give them money. The **government** are very worried about these 'sturdy beggars'. Some are armed with weapons, so be careful!

Finding out about clothes

Some Tudor clothes have lasted until the present day, but not many. Paintings tell us more about what people wore. There are more paintings of rich people. The rich could afford to pay artists to paint their families.

Life in the countryside

Most people live in the countryside. Many of them will never visit a town in their lives. Most travelling is on foot and the rough roads can be dangerous. Country life is very different from life in the cities. Most people work on the land but very few have their own farm. Instead, a rich landowner **rents** it out to them.

Most farmers have only enough land to be able to grow food for their families. To make things worse, rich landowners are throwing the farmers off their lands.

You might be invited to a feast. These people have dressed up for a special occasion.

Farmers use wooden ploughs, pulled by horses, to work the land.

They want to use the land for sheep farming because wool is very valuable. Landowners put fences around their new sheep farms. Many poor **peasant** farmers and farm workers have to become beggars.

Down on the farm

Wheat is grown to make bread, and barley is used to brew beer. People also grow vegetables. People are just starting to grow potatoes, which have been brought back from America by **explorers**. As well as sheep, pigs and cattle are farmed for their meat.

Eating and drinking

You will not have much choice about what you eat in Tudor England. Ordinary people have a very simple diet. They eat mainly bread and vegetables. Meat is expensive. Even the **peasant** farmers who keep animals do not eat meat very often. They sell their animals to earn money to pay the **rent**.

This is the type of thing you might find in a Tudor kitchen. There is no running water and the only heat comes from the fire.

Children and adults eat and drink the same things – even the beer and wine.

If you are lucky enough to eat some meat you will find it very salty. Salt is used to try and keep the meat fresh. There are no fridges in Tudor times. The water is dirty and might make you sick. Most people drink beer instead.

Finding out about feasts

Huge feasts were common among the rich. There was no shortage of meat for them. Queen Elizabeth's father, Henry VIII, was very famous for his feasts. In one year, the kitchens in his palace at Hampton Court cooked 8200 sheep and nearly 2000 pigs! Whole pigs or sheep were roasted on a spit over an open fire. Writings from the time tell us what was eaten in great houses.

Growing up

Babies are wrapped tightly in bandages called swaddling bands. These are supposed to make them grow straight and tall. Life for most children is hard. If you are poor, you will probably be sent to work when you are very young. You will have to work for about seven years as an **apprentice** to learn a trade, or skill. You may not even be paid during this time.

Many rich families employ an artist to paint the family portrait.

Children spend long days in the school room – from early morning until evening.

Going to school

The sons of wealthy families go to school. They go every day except Sunday, from early in the morning until five or six o'clock in the evening. The daughters of wealthy families do not usually go to school, but they may learn to read and write at home.

At school the boys will learn English, maths and Latin. Latin is the language the Romans used. It is used by all important people in Tudor times. You may find it hard to write neatly, however, as **quills** are used instead of pens. These are special feathers carefully trimmed and dipped in ink.

Having fun

There are plenty of different ways to relax in a Tudor town. You will find some of them very cruel. People pay to watch dogs attacking a bear at the bear-baiting. One favourite day out is going to watch criminals being **executed**. Football is played between whole villages. It is a very rough sport with lots of fighting between the teams.

Public executions are a form of entertainment in Tudor England. This drawing shows the famous execution of Elizabeth's cousin, Mary Queen of Scots.

The theatre

You might enjoy a trip to the theatre more. The most famous is the Globe Theatre in London. It is a round building and most of it has no roof. Plays are put on in the afternoon when there is plenty of light. You can pay a penny to stand on the floor. For 2 pennies, you can have a seat with a better view.

William Shakespeare

During Elizabethan times, William Shakespeare was the most famous playwright of them all. He wrote many famous plays, including romances such as *Romeo and Juliet*, comedies and plays about history. His plays were so good that people still go to see them today. They can tell us a lot about how Tudor people lived.

If you have enough pennies, you can go to the Globe Theatre to watch one of William Shakespeare's plays.

Sailors and explorers

If you visit the docks you will see sailors and **explorers** preparing for exciting journeys. They travel across the oceans in wooden ships. They risk their lives to find wealth and fame. In 1492, Christopher Columbus set sail from Spain. He discovered America – the New World. Spain became very rich from the gold and silver its explorers found.

If you pass by the docks you will probably see ships loading or unloading their goods.

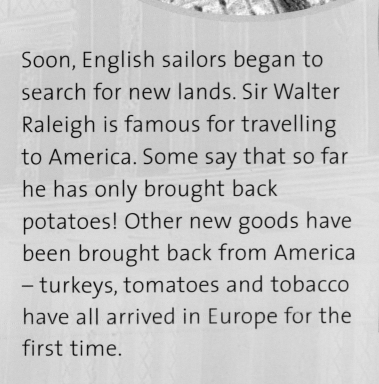

Soon, English sailors began to search for new lands. Sir Walter Raleigh is famous for travelling to America. Some say that so far he has only brought back potatoes! Other new goods have been brought back from America – turkeys, tomatoes and tobacco have all arrived in Europe for the first time.

Finding out about Sir Francis Drake

Sir Francis Drake (shown here) was another famous Tudor explorer. Between 1577 and 1580, he sailed around the world in his ship, the *Golden Hind*. The Spanish called him a pirate because he attacked their ships to steal gold. To the English, however, he was a hero. In 1588 he helped to defeat the Spanish Armada, which tried to invade England. There are many stories and pictures that tell us about Drake's life.

Art and technology

This is an exciting time for art and science. New ideas are spreading across Europe. This period of history is called the **Renaissance**, which means 'rebirth'. Artists and scientists are looking again at the ideas of the ancient Greeks and the Romans who lived more than 1000 years before them. Painters are beginning to make their pictures as lifelike as possible. Sometimes this can get them into trouble. Queen Elizabeth has ordered that any paintings of her that she does not like are to be destroyed.

There are no cameras in Tudor times, so wealthy people have their portraits painted instead.

Doctors are learning more and more. This doctor is teaching his students about the human body.

Inventions

Thanks to the **invention** of the printing press, people can read about ideas in printed books for the first time. Before this, all books were written by hand. Some inventions are very useful, for example the first flushing toilet. This was invented by an Englishman who tried to sell the idea to Queen Elizabeth, but it did not catch on for another 200 years.

Running the country

The most powerful person in the land is Queen Elizabeth. She has complete control of the country and chooses **government ministers**. The most powerful of these ministers form the Privy Council. They help run the country for the Queen.

There is also a **parliament**. The parliament has very little say in the running of the country. The Queen calls on parliament if she needs extra money. People have to pay **taxes** to raise this money.

Many people remember Elizabeth's father, King Henry VIII. He married six times and had three children, who all became monarchs.

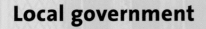

Queen Elizabeth and her ministers have to keep England safe from invasion by Spain. This painting shows the English fleet meeting the Spanish Armada.

Local government

A Justice of the Peace will be in charge of your local area. They look after everyday things such as repairing roads. They also judge criminals in court. There are no police. Local constables are chosen to track down criminals. They also have other jobs to do such as collecting taxes.

The Spanish Armada

Tudor England had many powerful enemies. King Philip II of Spain wanted to invade England because of a quarrel about religion. He sent a large fleet of ships, the Armada, to invade England in 1588. The English Navy defeated them. There are many paintings of this famous battle.

Tudor religion

All of England is Christian at this time. Everyone must follow the same religion as Queen Elizabeth. The religion followed is the **Church of England**. It has not always been like this. Until the time of Henry VIII, England was a **Roman Catholic** country. The **Pope** would not allow Henry to **divorce** his wife, so Henry made himself head of a new Church – the Church of England. He then allowed himself to divorce his wife.

Queen Mary believed that England should be a Catholic country.

Henry's daughter, Queen Mary, tried to make England a Catholic country again. When Elizabeth became Queen, however, the national religion changed back to the Church of England. Sometimes Catholics are treated cruelly. Many people have been killed because they do not have the same beliefs as the Queen.

Festivals

Life was hard for the Tudors, but people had the chance to enjoy lots of festivals. Everyone celebrated outside on May Day. People danced around a maypole. The twelve days of Christmas were also celebrated. All work stopped except for the looking after of animals.

Facts for Tudor times

Now you know a bit about Tudor England and its people. Here are a few other things you need to know to get by in Tudor times:

Money

Tudor money is divided into pounds (£), shillings (s) and pence (d). There are 12 pence in a shilling and 20 shillings in a pound.

A loaf of bread costs around half a penny.

Getting paid

In 1588, a law is passed in London fixing the wages of different trades:

- Clothworkers up to £5 per year

- Shoemakers up to £4 per year

- Butchers up to £6 per year

Population

In 1485, 2 million people lived in England. By the time of Queen Elizabeth's death, in 1603, the population is 4 million. England's biggest cities in 1600 are:

- London 200,000

- York 12,000

- Norwich 11,000

- Newcastle 10,000

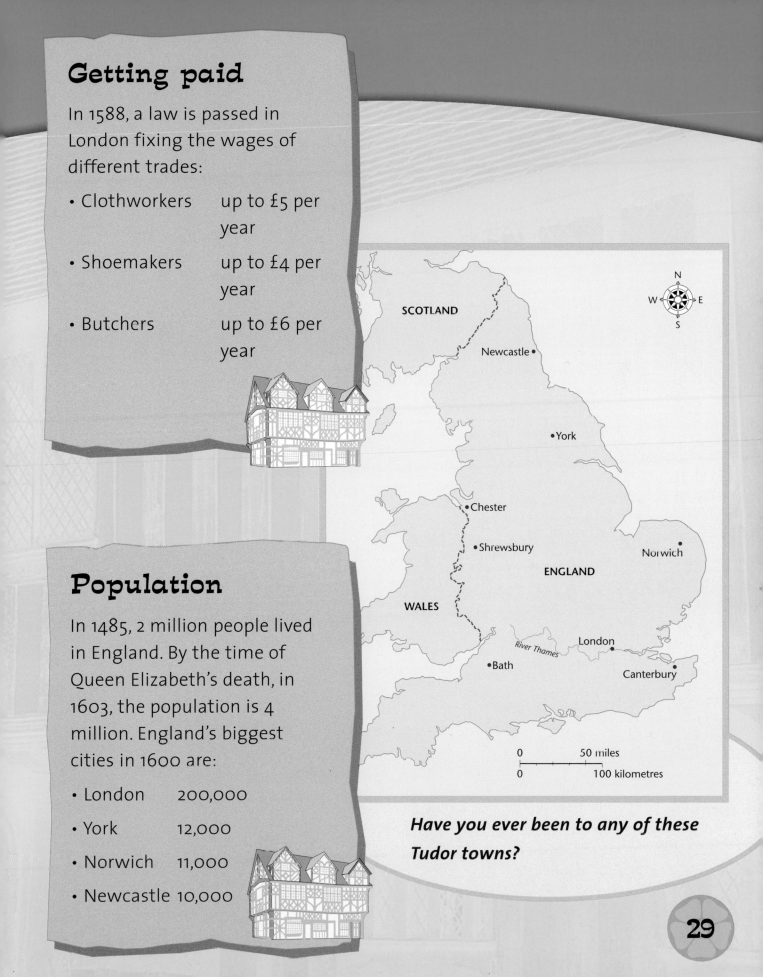

SCOTLAND

Newcastle •

• York

• Chester

• Shrewsbury

Norwich •

ENGLAND

WALES

River Thames

London

• Bath

Canterbury •

0 50 miles

0 100 kilometres

Have you ever been to any of these Tudor towns?

29

Find out for yourself

Unfortunately, you cannot travel back in time to Tudor England, but you can still find out lots about the people and how they lived. You will find the answers to some of your questions in this book. You can also use other books and the Internet.

Books to read

Britain Through the Ages: The Tudors, Felicity Hebditch (Evans Brothers, 2003)

How Do We Know About...?: The Defeat of the Spanish Armada, Deborah Fox (Heinemann Library, 2002)

On the Trail of the Tudors in Britain, Richard Wood (Franklin Watts, 1999)

Using the Internet

Explore the Internet to find out more about Tudor times. Websites can change, but if one of the links below no longer works, don't worry. Use a search engine such as www.yahooligans.com, and type in keywords such as 'Tudor', 'Shakespeare', 'Francis Drake' and 'Spanish Armada'.

Websites

http://www.brims.co.uk/tudors
Find plenty of useful information and a quiz.
http://www.bbc.co.uk/history/society_culture/society
Click on the 'Foul Facts Gallery' to find out more about the 'Terrible Tudors'.

Disclaimer
All the Internet addresses (URLs) given in this book were valid at the time of going to press. However, due to the dynamic nature of the Internet, some addresses may have changed, or sites may have ceased to exist since publication. While the author and publishers regret any inconvenience this may cause readers, no responsibility for any such changes can be accepted by either the author or the publishers

Glossary

apprentice   someone who is learning a trade or skill

barge   long boat with a flat bottom

breeches   trousers that reach down to around the knee

chamber pot   bowl kept in a bedroom, used as a toilet

Church of England   English religion that has the king or queen at its head

disease   illness

divorce   law that makes a couple no longer married

execute   kill someone as punishment for a crime

explorer   someone who travels to new lands for the first time

farthingale   hoop worn beneath a skirt to extend it out around the wearer

government   group of people who make decisions in parliament for the country

government minister   person who helps a king or queen rule

invention   something made or discovered for the first time

monarch   king or queen of a country

parliament   House of Lords and House of Commons, which meet in London to advise the king or queen

peasant   farmer or labourer who works on the land

poisonous   something containing a harmful substance

pope   head of the Catholic Church

quill   pen made by cutting a bird's feather to a point and dipping it in ink

Renaissance   time of discovery and exploration that changed the world between 1450 and 1650

rent   regular payment to a landowner by someone who uses the land

Roman Catholic   church that has the pope as its head

tax   money that has to be paid by everyone, in order to run the country

timber framed   building in which the frame is made of wood

vagabond   poor person or a beggar who turns to crime to get food

Index